PARTICIPANT'S GUIDE

Andy Stanley

ZONDERVAN®

NP
NORTH POINT
RESOURCES

ZONDERVAN.com/
AUTHORTRACKER
follow your favorite authors

ZONDERVAN

Faith, Hope, and Luck Participant's Guide
Copyright © 2009 by North Point Ministries, Inc.

Requests for information should be addressed to:
Zondervan, *Grand Rapids, Michigan 49530*

ISBN 978-0-310-32422-5

Cover and interior design by Brian Manley (funwithrobots.com)

Printed in the United States of America

13 14 15 • 24 23 22 21 20 19 18 17 16 15 14 13 12 11 10 9 8

CONTENTS

CAUSE AND EFFECT

by Andy Stanley

Faith, hope, luck — is there really any difference?

What's the cause-and-effect relationship between what *we* do and what *God* will do? Or is there one?

If you grew up in a Christian or a religious home, you were probably taught that God answers prayer. Maybe you were even taught that if you just had enough faith, God would say yes to your prayers. But how much faith is enough?

Too Incredible?

You may have met people who displayed incredible faith, and you thought, *I'd like to be like that.* And sometimes we hear people tell amazing stories of what their faith accomplished —they lost their job on Monday, said a few prayers on Tuesday, and by Wednesday got a call from a recruiter with a perfect job offer. Or the parents who have a rebellious son who runs away, so they get the church to pray. They send out an emergency email to get people all over the world to storm the gates of heaven. And within days, their son comes back—broken, crying, and ready for a fresh start. Or everybody's praying for the woman suddenly struck by cancer, and just before the scheduled surgery, they do one last X-ray and can't find anything—her tumor's gone. And that was seven years ago, and she's been healthy ever since.

Hey, those are the kinds of prayers we like!

But for most of us, it never quite works out that way. We know prayer is a part of the equation, and faith is part of the equation—but in your own life, you never see it all come together. Plus, when you poke around behind some of these amazing stories people tell, and they're honest, you find out that it didn't really work out perfectly for them either.

So our framework for faith—our everyday understanding of how God gets involved in our lives—tends to be a bit shaky. In fact, our faith is constantly reshaped by whatever happens to be going on in our lives. When things are going well, we feel good about the cool stuff God is doing; and when things are going badly, we think, *Where is God?* Our faith ebbs and flows based on our ability to see God at work in the present moment. And given life's randomness and toughness, our faith might eventually collapse. That's been the story for many people.

What then is the right lens through which to view our lives in relation to God and his involvement? What's the right foundation for faith? That's what we want to explore together in *Faith, Hope, and Luck.*

Trusting God? Or Just Hoping?

If you've been around Christians, you've probably heard some of them state with confidence that they're "trusting God" for something. But what's the difference between that and merely *hoping* for something? How can you realistically know God's going to do what you want him to? What's the real difference between just hoping for something and being able to say confidently, "I'm trusting God to do this"?

Meanwhile, we make decisions every day based on our current belief system, whatever that is. There's something propping up our assumptions about how the world works, about what God does or doesn't do for us. *Do you know what that is for you?*

These issues take on a special urgency when we encounter serious difficulties in life. Our prayers increase in quantity and urgency, but many times the same isn't true for the answers. That's when our faith—or lack of it—means everything. It can mean diving into knowing and enjoying God on a deeper level—or spiraling into emptiness and despair.

Such difficulties are inevitable, so it pays to explore these issues of faith — deliberately and thoroughly. We'll do that on the pages that follow . . .

BETTER ODDS

Do you have faith? Is your faith "working"? Does it match reality?

Maybe you've had to adjust your thinking about this over the years—perhaps many times. That's fine. Going through *Faith, Hope, and Luck* may bring even more changes for you.

We'll be exploring all this through the lens of Christianity. And we'll eventually take a look at something that makes Christianity different from all other religions and philosophies, including today's newer philosophies that can be very intriguing to learn about. We'll see a component in Christianity that makes it a more valid way to explore faith.

This exploration will be especially valuable if you're currently on the brink—or in the process—of abandoning your faith. You may feel that your world is coming apart, and you aren't sure what to think or what to pray. You don't know what to expect from God, or even if there is a God. We'll spend some time reflecting on some common reasons that happens.

DISCUSSION STARTER

How would you describe your overall philosophy of life—especially as it relates to how God interacts with human beings and intervenes in our circumstances? In your view, how does faith fit into all this?

VIDEO OVERVIEW

FOR SESSION 1 OF THE DVD

We hear amazing stories of faith from people who trusted God for something miraculous—then saw it happen. But in most of our lives, faith doesn't seem to work out like that. So how does faith really "work"?

This is a relevant issue regardless of our religious backgrounds or worldviews or philosophies of life, because we're all trying to figure out how life works based on our observations of everything around us, and there's always an element of faith in our approaches. So how does this faith thing really work, and where did it come from?

It's critical that we understand what we're leaning our faith against— what's propping it up. In other words, what's the real foundation of our faith or belief system?

When people abandon their faith, it's usually because of *lifestyle decisions* or *unexplainable circumstances*. Because of how we're living our lives, and how that conflicts with some standard or concept we once thought we believed in, we're forced to change our beliefs. Or we find that events and experiences in our lives can no longer be explained by how we've always thought of God and life, so we abandon or alter those beliefs and expectations.

Those scenarios indicate that our faith is *circumstantial*. To some extent, we all have an element of circumstantial faith—our beliefs are highly impacted by our own experiences and what we see around us.

Circumstantial faith, however, is fragile, because of the inconsistency and randomness we encounter in life. Besides, we aren't very good at interpreting these experiences; we're limited by our frames of reference (too short compared to God's) and by our inability to fully grasp what God's up to in our lives (too myopic compared to God's).

It's true that God sometimes uses significant events or circumstances in our lives to launch or jump-start our faith. But such "God moments" don't serve well as a continuing foundation. They, too, reflect a circumstantial faith.

Circumstantial faith will eventually fail us. At some point, it will become inconvenient, and we'll abandon or alter such faith in the face of temptations and pleasures. This only proves the continued insufficiency of this foundation for faith.

However, experience is *not* the foundation of Christianity. As we learn in Hebrews 4:14, we have something better than personal experience on which to base our faith. Scripture teaches us to base our faith

on Christ, who showed up in history 2,000 years ago to walk this earth
as one of us, who died on a cross, and who was resurrected from the
dead. This sets Christianity apart from all other religions.

So the foundation of our faith is *not* God's answers to our prayers,
or our experiences, or our ability to figure God out. The sure and last-
ing foundation of Christianity is a *person*—Jesus Christ, our Lord and
Savior.

VIDEO NOTES

_____

_____

_____

_____

_____

_____

_____

_____

_____

_____

_____

_____

_____

_____

_____

_____

_____

_____

_____

_____

DISCUSSION QUESTIONS

1. In your observation, what are the factors that cause people to abandon their faith? How would you describe the typical process that someone goes through in abandoning his or her faith?

2. To what degree is *your* faith shaped and influenced—or even controlled—by the circumstances of life?

3. When have you misinterpreted God's voice/direction? When have you been surprised or frustrated by God's time frame in answering your prayers?

4. What "God moments" have shaped your faith—events or experiences in which you felt God was especially present in your life?

5. In what instances or circumstances have you recognized that your faith is inconvenient, inadequate, or irrelevant?

6. Read Hebrews 12:2–3. These verses encourage us to rest our faith in the person and work of Jesus Christ. How is faith that rests in Jesus Christ different from faith that rests on our experiences?

MILEPOSTS

- Regardless of our backgrounds, worldviews, or philosophies of life, we all have belief systems that rest on something.

- At least to some extent, all of us have a faith that's circumstantial—shaped and determined by our personal experiences. Such circumstantial faith is fragile, and eventually it will fail us.

- Christianity, however, is based not on our experiences, but on a person—Jesus Christ—and the historical fact of his life, death, and resurrection 2,000 years ago. *He* is the reason we believe.

MOVING FORWARD

In Hebrews 4:14 we find the encouragement to hold tightly to our faith because of the fact of who Jesus is—our "great high priest." We're also encouraged to "fix our eyes on Jesus" (12:2). In practical terms, what would it mean for you this week to have your focus on Jesus instead of on your circumstances? When you "fix your eyes on Jesus"—what do you see? And how does that color your view of your circumstances?

CHANGING YOUR MIND

This session's key Scripture passage shifts our focus away from our circumstances and upward to where Jesus prays on our behalf. Let this be your steady encouragement this week:

*Therefore, since we have a great high priest
who has gone through the heavens,
Jesus the Son of God,
let us hold firmly to the faith we profess.*
Hebrews 4:14

PREPARATION FOR SESSION 2

To help you prepare for Session 2, use these suggested devotions during the week leading up to your small group meeting.

Day One

Look at the way faith is described in Hebrews 11:1–3. According to this passage, what are the most important things we should understand about faith? And how does this view of faith match your own experience?

Day Two

Read Hebrews 11:7, which tells us about the faith of Noah. Who or what initiated Noah's faith? And what seemed to be the process for how his faith developed?

Day Three

Look at the description of Abraham's faith in Hebrews 11:8–10. What seems to be the process of how faith developed in Abraham's life? What were the most significant aspects of his faith?

Day Four

What are the most important aspects of faith that we see in Hebrews 11:13? How did God's promises relate to their faith?

Day Five

Read Luke 5:12–13 and observe how this person approached Jesus. How did he demonstrate his faith? How would you describe his faith? And what more can we learn about faith from the way Jesus responded to this person?

Last Session

We all tend to have circumstantial faith—faith that's influenced by our circumstances and our personal observations of life. This kind of faith is fragile. But the Bible teaches that the true foundation for faith isn't experience, but a *person*. That person is Jesus Christ, who demonstrated by his life, death, and resurrection that he is God and came from God.

BETTING ON HOPE

We can get up every single day and fully rest our faith and confidence in God upon something that happened in *history*. We don't have to live life with our faith propped up only by our ability to see God in our present circumstances.

But what really is faith?

Since faith actually plays a part in how we approach life and on our perspectives of how the world works, there are endless ways to define faith. And thinking about it and discussing it can lead to confusion.

Maybe you've been told that if you just have enough faith, you can move a mountain. But the issue isn't the quantity of our faith. In fact, the object of our faith is much more important than the amount of faith we have. We can center our faith on the person of Jesus Christ, who is unchangeable. The strength of our faith won't ebb and flow based on our current circumstances. And by understanding what faith really *is*, we will open up our lives to the greatest practical benefit of practicing our faith day by day.

DISCUSSION STARTER

Faith can mean different things to different people. Identify the various components that you would include in a definition of faith. What belongs in the mix? And what doesn't belong?

VIDEO OVERVIEW

FOR SESSION 2 OF THE DVD

How do we define faith?

Even those who have been Christians for a long time sometimes wonder why God doesn't answer their prayers—why he doesn't come through for them. Sometimes others tell them, "It's because you don't have enough faith." But is that in line with what the Bible teaches?

There's something in all of us that wants to shrink God down to something we can control. True faith, however, involves something else. But first, consider what true faith is *not*.

Faith is not some force that allows us to pull God in our direction—where the more faith we have, the stronger our influence will be on God. The issue is not the *size* of your faith, but the *object* of your faith.

Faith is not some formula, like the combination to a lock. It's not doing enough of the right things in order to get God to do what you want him to do.

Faith is not the same as confidence, just as faith is not the same as hope. Nor is faith complicated. It is, in fact, extremely simple. We tend to complicate it out of our desire to manage God.

The Bible tells us (Hebrews 11:1) that "faith is being sure of what we hope for and certain of what we do not see." Faith is hope taken one step further. Faith means being sure of what we earlier had only hoped for.

This kind of faith "is what the ancients were commended for" (11:2); it's the proper view of faith that we see depicted and experienced throughout the Old and New Testaments, as men and women responded to God on the basis of what he had promised them.

God's promises are the bridge between hope and faith; they're what we can trust him for, with full assurance. Therefore, faith can be defined as the confidence that God is who he says he is and that he'll do everything he's promised to do.

This kind of faith is illustrated in Luke 5:12 by a man who approached Jesus. He "was covered with leprosy," his daily existence filled with affliction and misery. Seeing Jesus, this man fell on his face and begged, "Lord, if you are willing, you can make me clean." Seeing the man's faith, Jesus immediately touched him and healed him, as if to say, "That's all the faith I'm looking for. You recognized who I am and what I'm able to do, and you humbly asked."

VIDEO NOTES

_____

_____

_____

_____

_____

_____

_____

_____

_____

_____

_____

_____

_____

_____

_____

_____

_____

_____

_____

DISCUSSION QUESTIONS

1. In what ways have you tried to shrink God down to a manageable size in order to serve your desires?

2. Have you tended to view faith as (a) a quantifiable force, or (b) a formula? If you've seen faith as a force, what have you expected that force to accomplish? If you've seen faith as a formula, what are the components of the equation?

3. In your present understanding, how would you express the difference between *confidence, hope,* and *faith*?

4. Read Hebrews 11:1. The bridge from hope to faith is the promise or revelation of God. What are some promises from the Bible that have been especially meaningful to you?

5. What do you see as the right relationship between God's promises and our faith? How does this relationship work out in your life, especially in how you pray?

6. What are the things about your life and about God that you can be certain of?

MILEPOSTS

- Faith is not a force or a formula with which we can manage or manipulate God.

- Faith is not the same as confidence or hope. Nor is faith complicated. Faith is simply the confidence that God is who he says he is and that he'll do everything he's promised to do.

- Therefore, the promises of God are the bridge between our hope and our faith.

MOVING FORWARD

We tend to resist the biblical definition of faith because it takes faith out of our hands and puts God back in control. Much too often, we don't want God—we want a genie. But the goal of faith is not to get God to do what we want him to do; the goal of faith is to get us to live in accordance with the character and promises of God. Ultimately, faith comes down to trusting that God knows what he is doing. In what areas of your life is it difficult for you to believe that?

CHANGING YOUR MIND

Affix these words to the core of your personal understanding of faith:

Now faith is being sure of what we hope for
and certain of what we do not see.
Hebrews 11:1

PREPARATION FOR SESSION 3

To help you prepare for Session 3, use these suggested devotions during the week leading up to your small group meeting.

Day One

Review Hebrews 4:14, which we looked at in Session 1. Reflect on the personal meaning this passage has for you as a foundation for your faith. How significant is it to you that Jesus is your "great high priest"?

Day Two

Read the description of Jesus in Hebrews 2:17–18. How does this amplify the meaning of Jesus as our "high priest"? What practical benefit does this provide for you?

Day Three

Read Hebrews 4:15. What does this verse teach about Christ's personal understanding of your life? Why can Jesus empathize with you in every tough challenge you face?

Day Four

Read Hebrews 4:16. What are we clearly told to do in this passage, and what are we promised as a result? What does God's mercy mean to you? What does his grace include?

Day Five

Read Hebrews 10:19–25. How does this passage bring together many of the concepts we've been discussing in *Faith, Hope, and Luck*? What does a life of faith look like, according to this passage?

Last Session

Faith is simply the confidence that God is who he says he is and that he will do everything he's promised to do.

BEATING THE ODDS

As we continue to sort out how our ideas of God and faith operate in this world, our personal desires and wants enter the picture. We might crave inner peace, or a certain kind of relationship, or any number of things.

In light of those wants, when we embrace Christianity, what does God say he'll provide for us? If the promises of God are the bridge between our hope and our faith . . . then what exactly has God promised? In our day-to-day lives, what can we confidently expect God to give us and do for us?

Because he loves and cares for us, can we expect lives free from difficulty? God is the owner and source of all blessings and riches, so can we legitimately expect prosperity as we follow him? Jesus was a great healer, so can't we rightly expect perfect health?

As we look at what the Bible says about what God has truly promised us, we find greater clarity in answering these questions.

DISCUSSION STARTER

When you think of "God's promises," what first comes to mind? Do you think of his promises as being mostly unconditional, or conditional?

VIDEO OVERVIEW

FOR SESSION 3 of the DVD

Most of us would like God to fit in our back pockets or our backpacks as a modern-day genie who'll do what we want him to. But God can't be shrunk down to that . . . because God is God.

As we seek to learn how faith in God intersects with the real world, consider what happened to the very first followers of Jesus. Their lives were marked by suffering and persecution, and many were martyred. Their lives illustrate that God has *not* promised to keep bad things from happening to people who believe in him. Yet these believers continued to have extraordinary faith in Jesus.

God doesn't guarantee that his followers will have wealth or good health. Nor does he promise to reverse the negative consequences of our bad decisions. Sometimes God answers our prayers for such things as prosperity and healing. Sometimes he provides major relief from our bad decisions. But the Bible does not guarantee that kind of help. On the contrary, Jesus instead assures us, "In this world you will have trouble" (John 16:33).

So what *has* God promised to do for us?

When the writer of the book of Hebrews describes Jesus as our "great high priest" and encourages us to "hold firmly to the faith we profess" (4:14), he goes on to say, "For we do not have a high priest who is unable to sympathize with our weaknesses, but we have one who has been tempted in every way, just as we are—yet was without sin." Jesus, our Savior and Mediator and High Priest, fully understands everything we feel and everything we face. He knows, for example, what it's like to spend a night dreading the events of the following day. He knows what it is to experience the rejection and betrayal of those closest to him. He knows the crushing intensity of temptation.

Knowing this can radically change how we approach God, as the writer of Hebrews goes on to express: "Let us then approach the throne of grace with confidence, so that we may receive mercy and find grace to help us in our time of need" (4:16). We're to freely and unreservedly approach God in prayer for help in our time of need. And *mercy* and *grace* are what he promises to give us *every time*.

His mercy includes his compassionate understanding of our situations. And his grace includes the strength and ability to endure whatever difficulties we experience in our circumstances. He won't always deliver us *from* hardships, but he does promise to always deliver us *through* hardships, as we dependently trust in him.

VIDEO NOTES

DISCUSSION QUESTIONS

1. When you think of "God's promises," is it a long list or a short one? Which of God's promises, if any, seem to be the most important?

2. When it comes to health, wealth, and comfort, why do you think so many Christians develop wrong concepts and expectations regarding the promises of God?

3. What requests are appropriate to bring before God in prayer? Is anything and everything "fair game"?

4. Read Hebrews 4:14–16. God promises us mercy. How does Jesus' experience help us approach God with confidence?

5. Hebrews 4:14–16 also tells us that God promises mercy. Are mercy and grace tangible promises? How have you experienced God's mercy and grace?

6. How do these promises affect our ability to trust God during difficult times? Can it change the way we approach tough situations?

MILEPOSTS

- God has not promised his followers trouble-free lives, wealth, or perfect health.

- As we hold firmly to our faith, God encourages us to approach him in prayer—freely and confidently—in our times of need.

- Every time we approach him in this trustful dependence, God promises to give us mercy and grace. This grace includes the energy and ability to endure whatever difficult circumstances he has allowed into our lives.

MOVING FORWARD

At this time in your life, is there anything—any need, any anxiety, any concern, any crisis, any longing—that you've been hesitant to bring before God? Approach God's throne freely and with confidence, with his promise in Hebrews 4:16 as your motivation. In full and open dependence on him, open your life to his mercy and grace.

CHANGING YOUR MIND

God's throne is "the throne of grace"; let this promise motivate you to meet him there—more freely and more often:

Let us then approach the throne of grace
with confidence,
so that we may receive mercy
and find grace to help us
in our time of need.

Hebrews 4:16

PREPARATION FOR SESSION 4

To help you prepare for Session 4, use these suggested devotions during the week leading up to your small group meeting.

Day One

Read 2 Corinthians 12:1–6, where Paul mentions (in third person) a visionary experience in which for a time he was somehow connected with heavenly reality. Despite the exalted nature of such an experience, how does Paul indicate his weakness and his humility in these verses?

Day Two

In 2 Corinthians 12:7, Paul describes a severe affliction in his life. What do we learn in this verse about how Paul perceived the nature of this affliction and its source?

Day Three

Paul's response to his severe affliction is shown to us in 2 Corinthians 12:8. In what way was Paul approaching God's throne of grace "with confidence," in order to "receive mercy and find grace to help" in his time of need (Hebrews 4:16)?

Day Four

In 2 Corinthians 12:9, we see God's response to Paul's repeated prayer. No physical relief for Paul's affliction was provided; something else was promised. What was it? Was it better than what Paul asked for? In what way did Paul "receive mercy and find grace to help" in his time of need (Hebrews 4:16)?

Day Five

Read 2 Corinthians 12:9–10 and think about how Paul responded to God's answer to his prayer. How does Paul's experience and perspective here relate to your own life? What guidance does this offer in your own response to any continuing hardships in your life?

Last Session

What has God promised to do for us? His promises are the bridge between our hope and our faith. We can have absolute confidence that he'll do what he says—he'll always give us what he promises. And his promises include his mercy and grace for our time of need whenever we confidently and trustingly pray to him.

NO DICE

What happens when you feel like God is saying no to the legitimate requests you make? Or when you sense there's no answer at all?

You ask . . . silence . . . and nothing changes.

DISCUSSION STARTER

What would you say are the most common ways that people respond to severe hardship in their lives? What seem to be the most common patterns in how they deal with it? *How do you deal with it?*

VIDEO OVERVIEW

FOR SESSION 4 of the DVD

Receiving God's "no" in answer to our prayers can be devastating. It can crush our faith.

But it doesn't have to, as Paul's example demonstrates in 2 Corinthians 12. A man of extraordinary faith, Paul had become the leading advocate for Christianity in the first-century Roman Empire, and his ministry had astonishing impact.

But along with this ministry success, the Bible tells us that God gave Paul some sort of acute affliction to keep him from becoming proud or arrogant. This affliction was apparently noticeable and perhaps even offensive to others Paul was around. Paul called it "a thorn in my flesh, a messenger of Satan, to torment me" (12:7).

Paul desperately pleaded, in three different times of extended prayer, for God to remove this burdensome affliction. God, however, did not grant Paul relief.

Instead, Paul received this personal answer from God: "My grace is sufficient for you, for my power is made perfect in weakness" (12:9). Through Paul's inescapable weakness, God intended to "show off"— people would be astounded that Paul, despite such a limitation, would proclaim the gospel with authority and effectiveness, and God's presence and power would be the only explanation for it. Therefore, Paul could respond, "That is why, for Christ's sake, I delight in weaknesses, in insults, in hardships, in persecutions, in difficulties. For when I am weak, then I am strong" (12:10).

Paul decided to stop asking God to remove his affliction, and he instead accepted it as a lifelong burden. He learned to boast in this continuing weakness, so that Christ's power would rest on him.

It can also be that way for us: In the midst of something we can't control or change, *our greatest weaknesses become God's greatest opportunities to show himself strong in our lives.*

This kind of empowered grace is offered to us only as we're truly depending on God. In fact, it takes more faith to endure a no from God than to receive a yes.

As we face our most demanding trials, we don't really want a God who sits in our back pockets. Instead, we want a sovereign, powerful, omniscient God, one who's vastly bigger than us—yet who intimately loves us and sent his Son to die for us.

We want a God who allows sin to have consequences—yet who also understands our pain and weaknesses. And because of the sufficiency of his grace, as we continue to trust him, he gives us unexplainable strength to endure even when he says no to our prayers.

If we instead respond to his "no" by essentially shaking our fists at him, we miss his full grace; we'll instead face even worse complications and difficulties. But even then, we can come back to God in brokenness and find his grace again.

VIDEO NOTES

_____

_____

_____

_____

_____

_____

_____

_____

_____

_____

_____

_____

_____

_____

_____

_____

_____

_____

_____

_____

DISCUSSION QUESTIONS

1. What is your typical pattern for responding to tough circumstances in your life?

2. To what degree do you think God brings hardships into our lives in order to curb our pride and strengthen our humility? How effective is this?

3. As you consider Paul's words in 2 Corinthians 12:7–10, what seemed to be the most important considerations in God's mind and heart as he dealt with Paul in this situation?

4. Read Philippians 4:6. God invites us to bring our requests to him. Why does God invite us to pray when his response is oftentimes no?

5. What are the toughest circumstances in your life that seem to fall under the category of negative conditions that are not likely to change?

6. What are some practical ways in which our weaknesses serve as vehicles for God's grace and glory to be better evidenced and experienced (as Paul experienced in 2 Corinthians 12:9–10)?

MILEPOSTS

- Sometimes we plead with God for something, and we commit to change our lives—if only he'll say yes to our prayers. But when he gives us what we want, we seldom go on to experience significant life change.

- When we plead with God for something and his answer is no, he still offers us the power, grace, and endurance to keep on going in spite of difficult circumstances.

- The point of greatest weakness in your life at this moment is God's greatest opportunity—if you'll trust him.

MOVING FORWARD

What is a difficult situation in your life right now—one specific circumstance—in which you sense that God is asking you to trust him? How do you foresee that you can more fully experience his grace and power in this situation? How can you genuinely affirm, "I will boast all the more gladly about my weaknesses, so that Christ's power may rest on me" (2 Corinthians 12:9)? How will you be able to truly say, "When I am weak, then I am strong" (12:10)?

CHANGING YOUR MIND

Take the following words of the Lord to Paul—as well as Paul's heart response to those words—as your own personal guidance from God in enduring your life's toughest challenges:

But he said to me,
"My grace is sufficient for you,
for my power is made perfect in weakness."
Therefore I will boast all the more gladly
about my weaknesses,
so that Christ's power may rest on me.

2 Corinthians 12:9

PREPARATION FOR SESSION 5

To help you prepare for Session 5, use these suggested devotions during the week leading up to your small group meeting.

Day One

Read the words of Jesus in John 5:30. What can you learn about his goals and purposes for his ministry and life—and how do they compare with your own?

Day Two

Read the words of Jesus in John 6:38–39. What can you learn from them about his goals and purposes for his ministry and life—and how do they compare with your own?

Day Three

Read the words of Jesus in John 12:49–50. What do they reveal about his goals and purposes for his life—and how do they compare with yours?

Day Four

Read the words of Jesus in John 14:10–13. What exactly is Jesus promising his followers in the last two verses? And how does this relate to your life?

Day Five

Read 1 John 5:14–15. What does this promise from God mean to you personally?

Last Session

God allows serious hardships in our lives as a means for us to more fully experience his power and grace as we continue to endure. As we continue to trust him, we learn that our points of greatest weakness are also God's greatest opportunities.

ALL IN

We can lean heavily into God's grace in our time of need. Every time we come to him, we can experience his presence, and he has promised to give us his grace and mercy whenever we do.

Even when he says no to our heartfelt requests, and even when we experience pain and trauma in our lives, those are the arenas in which God can do his greatest work.

Faith isn't about escaping tough circumstances or avoiding pain. Faith is simply waking up each day and saying, "God, you're great, and I trust you; and my faith is going to be manifested in this world as I surrender to your direction."

That kind of surrender gets us in sync with what God is doing in our world. And it makes possible for us the greatest degree of life-change.

DISCUSSION STARTER

Who would you point to as the best examples of extraordinary faith—those whose faith seems stronger than anyone else's? What is it about their lives and faith that stands out the most to you?

VIDEO OVERVIEW

FOR SESSION 5 of the DVD

What does it look like to have *great* faith—big, extraordinary, amazing faith?

It's clear in the New Testament that Jesus was a man of extraordinary faith. But this wasn't something he leveraged to serve his own agenda. Instead, this man of extraordinary faith was also extraordinarily surrendered to his Father in heaven.

Throughout the Bible, in fact, we see that great faith means great surrender.

If we fully embrace that the sovereign, all-knowing, all-powerful God loves us enough to send his Son into this world to die for our sins, our logical response to him is not "What can you do for me?" but "How can I serve you?" The logical response is absolute, total surrender. Your authenticity in following Jesus Christ will be revealed most clearly *not* in getting God to do what you want him to do, but in how much you surrender to his will.

We see this emphatically in the life of Jesus. Even with all his power and goodness, he didn't pursue his own plans and goals, or work in his own way (John 5:30; 12:49–50). He was a simple man with a simple plan.

Jesus didn't come here to initiate his own program or to carry out his own ideas (John 6:38). He took all his cues from his Father in heaven. Why? Because he had extraordinary faith. He believed that the Father is who the Father says he is. And if there is a God like him for us to trust, why would we show up with our own agendas?

We also learn from Jesus that God's will is about *other people* (John 6:39). God's will for us requires a selfless agenda. It's like being a vessel or vehicle or pipeline through which God can do his work on behalf of other people.

That's where Jesus was coming from. That's the backdrop to keep in mind when we read his statements, such as this one in John 14:12: "I tell you the truth, anyone who has faith in me will do what I have been doing. He will do even greater things than these, because I am going to the Father." The "greater things" will spring from a fully surrendered faith, and they will not be for our own benefit, but for the benefit of others.

This calls for us to get on our knees and ask God, "What's next? What do you want me to do and to say? Where do you want me to go?"

And when Jesus promises, "I will do whatever you ask in my name, so that the Son may bring glory to the Father" (John 14:13), it isn't about launching new ideas and asking God to get involved with them. It's about surrendering to God by saying, "What do you want done in my world, in my relationships, in my finances, in my work, in my community?"

We also see this in God's promise (1 John 5:14–15) that "he hears us" when we "ask anything according to his will"; and knowing that he hears us—"whatever we ask"—we can also know that "we have what we asked of him."

Therefore, we're to spend our lives trying to discern God's plan for us and our world, and then get in line with what God wants done.

VIDEO NOTES

_____

_____

_____

_____

_____

_____

_____

_____

_____

_____

_____

_____

_____

_____

_____

_____

_____

_____

_____

_____

_____

_____

DISCUSSION QUESTIONS

1. What areas of your life are you unwilling to surrender to God?

2. From God's perspective, what's the proper place in our lives for personal goals and plans?

3. Read John 12:49–50. Why does Jesus surrender so willingly to his Father? Is this a passive response? Why is surrendering control so hard for people?

4. Why does experiencing brokenness or weakness help so many people come to faith in Jesus?

5. In John 14:12, Jesus promised that his followers would do "even greater things" than he did in life. What do you think those "greater things" might be for you?

6. As a result of studying *Faith, Hope, and Luck*, what changes have you seen in your view of God, of faith, and of yourself?

MILEPOSTS

- Great faith means great surrender. Our logical response to all that God has done for us is not "What can you do for me?" but "How can I serve you?"

- The portrait of Jesus in the New Testament reveals a man of great faith who was fully surrendered to God's will and God's work, with no agenda of his own. That should also be true of us.

- It's an insult to God for us to try to use him merely to help us get whatever we want out of life and to feel better about ourselves.

MOVING FORWARD

Faith is not about moving God to embrace our agendas. It is about being moved to embrace his agenda. As Jesus demonstrates for us, great faith is reflected in great surrender. Lots of people come to this place of surrender on their own or as a result of broken seasons in their lives. Either way, yielding control of our lives to God invites him to come alive in us in ways that help us reach our full potential.

As an exercise this week, start your days by praying, "I'm going to live as if you are who you say you are and will do everything you have promised to do. Let your will be done in my life."

CHANGING YOUR MIND

Hold on to this promise from Jesus as you live in pursuit of God's agenda and purposes—and doing everything God's way:

I tell you the truth,
anyone who has faith in me
will do what I have been doing.
He will do even greater things than these,
because I am going to the Father.
And I will do whatever you ask in my name,
so that the Son may bring glory to the Father.

John 14:12–13

LEADER'S GUIDE

So, you're the leader...

Is that intimidating? Perhaps exciting? No doubt you have some mental pictures of what it will look like, what you will say, and how it will go. Before you get too far into the planning process, there are some things you should know about leading a small group discussion. We've compiled some proven techniques to help you.

BASICS ABOUT LEADING

1. Cultivate discussion — It's easy to think that the meeting lives or dies by your ideas. In reality, the ideas of everyone in the group are what make a small group meeting successful. The most valuable thing you can do is to get people to share their thoughts. That's how the relationships in your group will grow and thrive. Here's a rule: The impact of your study material will typically never exceed the impact of the relationships through which it was studied. The more meaningful the relationships, the more meaningful the study. In a sterile environment, even the best material is suppressed.

2. Point to the material — A good host or hostess gets the party going by offering delectable hors d'oeuvres and beverages. You too should be ready to serve up "delicacies" from the material. Sometimes you will simply read the discussion questions and invite everyone to respond. At other times, you may encourage others to share their ideas. Remember, some of the best treats are the ones your guests bring to the party. Go with the flow of the meeting, and be ready to pop out of the kitchen as needed.

3. Depart from the material — A talented ministry team has carefully designed this study for your small group. But that doesn't mean you should follow every part word for word. Knowing how and when to depart from the material is a valuable art. Nobody knows more about your people than you do. The narratives, questions, and exercises are here to provide a framework for discovery. However, every group is motivated differently. Sometimes the best way to start a small group discussion is simply to ask, "Does anyone have a personal insight or revelation you'd like to share from this week's material?" Then sit back and listen.

4. Stay on track — Conversation is like the currency of a small group discussion. The more interchange, the healthier the "economy." However, you need to keep your objectives in mind. If your goal is to have a meaningful experience with this material, then you should make sure the discussion is contributing to that end. It's easy to get off on a tangent. Be prepared to interject politely and refocus the group. You may need to say something like, "Excuse me, we're obviously all interested in this subject; however, I just want to make sure we cover all the material for this week."

5. Above all, pray — The best communicators are the ones that manage to get out of God's way enough to let him communicate *through* them. That's important to keep in mind. Books, sermons, and group discussions don't teach God's Word. God himself speaks into the hearts of men and women, and prayer is our vital channel to communicate directly with him. Cover your efforts in prayer. You don't just want God present at your meetings; you want him to direct them.

We hope you find these suggestions helpful. And we hope you enjoy leading this study. You will find additional guidelines and suggestions for each session in the Leader's Guide notes that follow.

LEADER'S GUIDE
SESSION NOTES

SESSION 1 — BETTER ODDS

Bottom Line

We all tend to have circumstantial faith—faith that's colored by our circumstances and our personal observations of life. Unfortunately, this kind of faith is fragile. But the Bible teaches that the true foundation for faith isn't experience, but a *person*. That person is Jesus Christ, who demonstrated by his life, death, and resurrection that he is God and came from God.

Discussion Starter

Use the "Discussion Starter" printed in Session 1 of the Participant's Guide to "break the ice"—and to help everyone see that we're all working on our approaches to life (and our understanding of God) and that the exercise of faith is always part of it.

Notes for Discussion Questions

1.   **In your observation, what are the factors that cause people to abandon their faith? How would you describe the typical process that someone goes through in abandoning his or her faith?**

      Use this question to help everyone understand the real and present danger—which the Bible addresses—of failing to hold fast to our faith.

2.   **To what degree is *your* faith shaped and influenced—or even controlled—by the circumstances of life?**

      Answering this honestly should help everyone see that we all tend to let our faith be colored by our circumstances and life observations.

3.   **When have you misinterpreted God's voice/direction? When have you been surprised or frustrated by God's time frame in answering your prayers?**

      The responses to this question should help your group see the spectrum of answers to prayer—from a definitive YES! from God to an eerily silent no.

4.   **What "God moments" have shaped your faith—events or experiences in which you felt God was especially present in your life?**

These answers are likely to bring up some strong emotions and memories.

5.   **In what instances have you recognized that your faith is inconvenient, inadequate, or irrelevant?**

Spend a generous amount of discussion time to uncover these moments of vulnerability. For some, these may be the kinds of memories we've tried to forget.

6.   **Read Hebrews 12:2–3. These verses encourage us to rest our faith in the person and work of Jesus Christ. How is faith that rests in Jesus Christ different from faith that rests on our experiences?**

The foundation of true Christian faith is not *experience*, but a *person*. This is the key point of Session 1. Encourage everyone to bring in Scriptures they know that communicate and reinforce this core truth.

Moving Forward

The goal is to help your group look increasingly to Jesus as the "author and perfecter" of their personal faith (Hebrews 12:2).

Preparation for Session 2

Remember to point out the brief daily devotions that the group members can complete. They will help stimulate discussion in your next session. These devotions will enable everyone to dig into the Bible and start wrestling with the topics that will come up next time.

SESSION 2 — BETTING ON HOPE

Bottom Line

We need a clear definition of faith. Here it is: faith is simply the *confidence that God is who he says he is and that he will do everything he's promised to do.*

Discussion Starter

Use the "Discussion Starter" listed for this session in the Participant's Guide. This one should help everyone in your group see that we have various ideas about what faith involves.

Notes for Discussion Questions

1. **In what ways have you tried to shrink God down to a manageable size in order to serve your desires?**

    Share your own honest response, and encourage everyone to do the same.

2.   **Have you tended to view faith as a (a) quantifiable force, or (b) a formula? If you've seen faith as a force, what have you expected that force to accomplish? If you've seen faith as a formula, what are the components of the equation?**

Most of us have times when we tend to come up with our own "formulas" for faith. Look to the past as well as the present for answers to this question.

3.   **In your present understanding, how would you express the difference between *confidence, hope,* and *faith?***

Also bring in the perspectives taught in the DVD content on this topic.

4.   **Read Hebrews 11:1. The bridge from hope to faith is the promise or revelation of God. What are some promises from the Bible that have been especially meaningful to you?**

Give everyone in your group an opportunity to respond to this question. As a result, you may develop a sense of your group members' familiarity with the Bible and how they view God.

5.   **What do you see as the right relationship between God's promises and our faith? How does this relationship work out in your life, especially in how you pray?**

The goal is to work to build up a stronger dependence on God's trustworthy promises.

6.   **What are the things about your life and about God that you can be certain of?**

Help guide the discussion toward God's explicit promises and the truths of Scripture.

Moving Forward

Encourage your group members to realize that they can freely approach God in prayer *because of who he is.* Encourage them to focus on him, not on themselves, and not on what he can do for them as they come to him in open and honest prayer.

Preparation for Session 3

Again, encourage your group members to complete the brief daily devotions. These will help stimulate discussion in your next session. They'll enable everyone to dig into the Bible and start wrestling with the topics coming up next time.

SESSION 3 — BEATING THE ODDS

Bottom Line

What has God promised to do for us? His promises are the bridge between our hope and our faith. We can have absolute confidence that he'll do what he says—he'll always give us what he promises. And his promises include his mercy and grace for our times of need whenever we confidently and trustingly pray to him.

Discussion Starter

Again, use the "Discussion Starter" listed for this session in the Participant's Guide. Identify and summarize the perspectives and assumptions your group holds regarding God's promises.

Notes for Discussion Questions

1. **When you think of "God's promises," is it a long list or a short one? Which of God's promises, if any, seem to be the most important?**

   Help everyone see the crucial importance of the gospel and its rich and full promise of salvation through Christ.

2.   **When it comes to health, wealth, and comfort, why do you think so many Christians develop wrong concepts and expectations regarding the promises of God?**

Unwise and unhealthy teaching is certainly a factor here, but so is our quick and selfish readiness to believe it.

3.   **What requests are appropriate to bring before God in prayer? Is anything and everything "fair game"?**

Help guide the discussion to the truth that we're free to bring all our requests before God, whatever they are.

4.   **Read Hebrews 4:14–16. God promises us mercy. How does Jesus' experience help us approach God with confidence?**

You can also ask a follow-up question such as: How can Jesus, who lived in the first century, fully understand what we're experiencing today?

5.   **Hebrews 4:14–16 also tells us that God promises mercy. Are mercy and grace tangible promises? How have you experienced God's mercy and grace?**

Challenge your group members to explore in depth the ideas of grace and mercy and how those concepts have tangibly been reflected in their lives.

6.   **How do these promises affect our ability to trust God during difficult times? Does it change the way we approach tough situations?**

Spend enough time to recognize the infinite richness and fullness of God's mercy and grace toward us.

Moving Forward

Help your group members understand that they can approach God freely and confidently in prayer with whatever needs and concerns they have. Help them see how much God values their coming before him with honest recognition of their neediness.

Preparation for Session 4

Again, encourage your group members to complete the daily devotions. This will help them be better prepared for the topics coming up next time.

SESSION 4 — NO DICE

Bottom Line

God allows serious hardships in our lives as a means for us to more fully experience his power and grace as we continue to endure. We learn that our points of greatest weakness are also God's greatest opportunities, as we trust him.

Discussion Starter

Again, use the "Discussion Starter" listed for this session in the Participant's Guide. There may be a wide variety of answers. Later, the discussion questions will direct your group members to think more personally about their responses to hardship.

Notes for Discussion Questions

1. **What is your typical pattern for responding to tough circumstances in your life?**

    This may be something that many of us fail to recognize in ourselves. Allow enough time to bring out the truth.

2. **To what degree do you think God brings hardships into our lives in order to curb our pride and strengthen our humility? How effective is this?**

   We see this in Paul's example in 2 Corinthians 12, but also in other biblical contexts—as well as in our own lives.

3. **As you consider Paul's words in 2 Corinthians 12:7–10, what seemed to be the most important considerations in God's mind and heart as he dealt with Paul in this situation?**

   Look especially at the factors of God's glory and the display and free flow of his grace.

4. **Read Philippians 4:6. God invites us to bring our requests to him. Why does God invite us to pray when his response is oftentimes no?**

   You can ask your group members about specific situations where they felt they received a no from God.

5. **What are the toughest circumstances in your life that seem to fall under the category of negative conditions that are not likely to change?**

   There may be significant reluctance to fully identify these. The main point is to help each person clearly recognize the answer for himself or herself.

6. **What are some practical ways in which our weaknesses serve as vehicles for God's grace and glory to be better evidenced and experienced (as Paul experienced in 2 Corinthians 12:9–10)?**

This will again bring out the open recognition of their biggest weaknesses, if the group is comfortable enough with each other to share these things.

Moving Forward

Again, look strongly to Paul's example in handling life's most difficult and long-lasting hardships.

Preparation for Session 5

Once more, encourage your group members to complete the daily devotions in preparation for the next session.

SESSION 5 — ALL IN

Bottom Line

Great faith means great surrender—as especially demonstrated in the life of Jesus. Our logical response to all that God has done for us would not be "What can you do for me?" but "How can I serve you?"

Discussion Starter

Once more, use the "Discussion Starter" listed for this session in the Participant's Guide. Encourage the group members to say more about the degree of commitment, sacrifice, and surrender they've noticed in the lives of those whom they identify as having "extraordinary faith."

Notes for Discussion Questions

1. **What areas of your life are you unwilling to surrender to God?**

    Your group members' responses could provide opportunities to incorporate some accountability among your group.

2.   **From God's perspective, what's the proper place in our lives for personal goals and plans?**

Help everyone recognize the crucial importance of submitting and yielding our personal pursuits to God's higher intentions.

3.   **Read John 12:49–50. Why does Jesus surrender so willingly to his Father? Is this a passive response? Why is surrendering control so hard for people?**

Allow your group members to discuss the difference between active and passive responses. Challenge those in your group to reconsider what "surrender" means if they believe it to be a weak act of faith.

4.   **Why does experiencing brokenness or weakness help so many people come to faith in Jesus?**

This is a question that can trigger group members to remember their own journeys of faith, since so many people start their relationship with Jesus Christ in response to a low point in their lives.

5.   **In John 14:12, Jesus promised that his followers would do "even greater things" than he did in life. What do you think**

those "greater things" might be for you?

Encourage everyone here to look closely at the life and char-

acter of Jesus.

6.   **As a result of studying *Faith, Hope, and Luck*, what changes**

have you seen in your view of God, of faith, and of yourself?

Allow plenty of time for a thorough review of this study course

and its degree of helpfulness for everyone in your group.

Moving Forward

There may be a need to release personal goals and agendas in light

of God's greater purposes. Encourage everyone in your group to be

open to this.

Share Your Thoughts

With the Author: Your comments will be forwarded to the author when you send them to *zauthor@zondervan.com*.

With Zondervan: Submit your review of this book by writing to *zreview@zondervan.com*.

Free Online Resources at

www.zondervan.com

Zondervan AuthorTracker: Be notified whenever your favorite authors publish new books, go on tour, or post an update about what's happening in their lives.

Daily Bible Verses and Devotions: Enrich your life with daily Bible verses or devotions that help you start every morning focused on God.

Free Email Publications: Sign up for newsletters on fiction, Christian living, church ministry, parenting, and more.

Zondervan Bible Search: Find and compare Bible passages in a variety of translations at www.zondervanbiblesearch.com.

Other Benefits: Register yourself to receive online benefits like coupons and special offers, or to participate in research.

ZONDERVAN®
.com